# Machines with Power!

# Trains

by Amy McDonald

BELLWETHER MEDIA
MINNEAPOLIS, MN

**Blastoff! Beginners** are developed by literacy experts and educators to meet the needs of early readers. These engaging informational texts support young children as they begin reading about their world. Through simple language and high frequency words paired with crisp, colorful photos, Blastoff! Beginners launch young readers into the universe of independent reading.

Blastoff! Universe

Reading Level — Grade K

Grades 1-3

Grade 4

## Sight Words in This Book 🔍

| | | |
|---|---|---|
| a | many | they |
| all | on | this |
| are | people | under |
| go | the | where |
| is | there | would |
| it | these | you |

This edition first published in 2021 by Bellwether Media, Inc.

No part of this publication may be reproduced in whole or in part without written permission of the publisher. For information regarding permission, write to Bellwether Media, Inc., Attention: Permissions Department, 6012 Blue Circle Drive, Minnetonka, MN 55343.

Library of Congress Cataloging-in-Publication Data

LC record for Trains available at https://lccn.loc.gov/2020007091

Text copyright © 2021 by Bellwether Media, Inc. BLASTOFF! BEGINNERS and associated logos are trademarks and/or registered trademarks of Bellwether Media, Inc.

Editor: Christina Leaf    Designer: Andrea Schneider

Printed in the United States of America, North Mankato, MN.

# Table of Contents

# What Are Trains?

All aboard!
Hop on the train!

Trains are machines. They travel on **tracks**.

tracks

**Engineers** drive trains. They control the speed.

engineer

# Parts of a Train

This is the **engine**.
It pulls the train.

engine

These are
the wheels.
They move
along the tracks.

wheels

These are
train cars.
There are
many kinds.

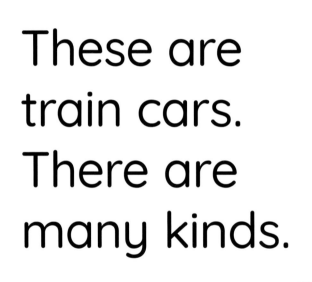

tank car

726171

train cars

hopper car

boxcar

30 89

15

# Trains at Work

This is a
**freight train.**
It carries goods.

goods

This is a subway.
It moves under
the ground!

This train carries people. Where would you go?

# Train Facts

## Train Parts

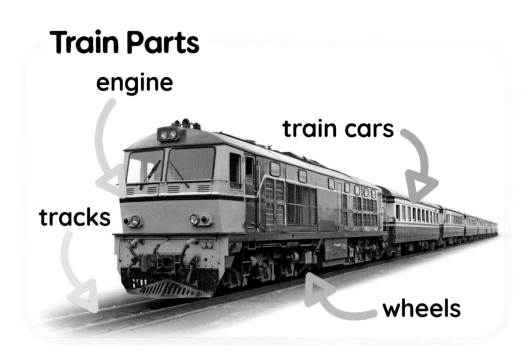

engine

train cars

tracks

wheels

## Types of Train Cars

tank car

boxcar

hopper car

# Glossary

**engine**

the car that pulls a train

**engineers**

people who drive trains

**freight train**

a train that carries goods

**tracks**

the path for a train

# To Learn More

## ON THE WEB

# FACTSURFER

Factsurfer.com gives you a safe, fun way to find more information.

1. Go to www.factsurfer.com.

2. Enter "trains" into the search box and click .

3. Select your book cover to see a list of related content.

# Index

24